THE GRAVITY OF QUIET

77 HAIKUS CELEBRATING THE BEAUTY OF EVERYDAY LIFE

SNEHA CHANDRASHEKAR

Clever Fox®
PUBLISHING
Chennai • Bangalore

CLEVER FOX PUBLISHING
Chennai, India

Published by CLEVER FOX PUBLISHING 2026

Paperback ISBN: 978-93-7500-003-7
Hardback ISBN: 978-93-7500-311-3

In remembrance of my mother, whose grace taught me to seek the gentle miracles hidden in everyday stillness.

To P, whose quiet strength, patience, and love have been the soft ground beneath every step of my becoming.

To A, Champagne, and Merlot, you are my daily magic, my chaos, my constants, and the heartbeats of my world.

Fuzzy clouds of joy

A singular promise blooms

Love's soft endless glow

– S

On what the world orbits around, love…

GRATITUDE FOR THESE VOICES

The Gravity of Quiet is a work of gentle beauty, celebrating the profound depth of everyday life and universal human experience. Through seventy-seven poignant haikus, the author, Sneha, draws us out of the chaos of the modern world and into the much-needed stillness of reflection. These poems will calm and move you, and their soft echoes will stay with you long after you turn the page.

– Esfandiar Ghodrati

Author of Mindsweeper and Legend Has It

Film Producer • Philanthropist

I have known Sneha as someone who listens deeply—to people, to ideas, and to the spaces in between. The Gravity of Quiet carries that same quality of attention. These haikus are not written to impress; they are written from stillness. Reading this book feels like sitting beside a friend who gently points you back to what you already know but have forgotten to notice—the softness of a morning, the weight of a memory, the intelligence of silence. In a time that constantly pulls us outward, this book does the rare work of returning us inward. It is not meant to be rushed through, but lived with—one page, one pause, one breath at a time.

– Rajiv Talreja

International Bestselling Author - Lead or Bleed

WHISPERS FROM THE POET

Haiku, for me, is the most soulful expression of my being, a quiet doorway into the beauty of simply noticing. A doorway where the ordinary softens, the veil thins, and the world reveals its quiet secrets. In its brevity, I find a vastness; in its stillness, a pulse.

The slow ache of everyday mundanity, the soft swell of emotions, the hidden architecture of the universe, all of it breathes beneath the surface of our ordinary days, waiting to be noticed.

There is a sacredness in the way your cat watches you before dawn breaks, as if it remembers a truth you've forgotten. The way each morning unfolds with an ancient precision, as though time itself is gently resetting the cosmos on your behalf. The love you offer with a glance, a gesture, a word, becomes its own kind of alchemy, reshaping the air around those you hold dear.

Even the tight pull of disappointment or grief, that subtle twitch in your stomach, is an intricate art of being alive, worthy of reverence.

Through these 77 haikus, I've tried to honour fleeting truths, the little moments, the quiet discoveries, the tender revelations that make up a life. May you walk through these pages as you would through a quiet forest at dusk, and you fall in love with your own life more deeply, truly, and intently.

THE GRAVITY OF QUIET – THE INTRODUCTION

Seventy-seven haikus. Six movements. One quiet, unfolding journey.

This collection traces the arc of being from the grounding rhythms of **Nature**, through the warmth and ache of **Love**, into the dark valleys of **Shadows**, rising again in the fire of **Creation**, expanding into the vast mystery of the **Universe**, and finally arriving at the soft embrace of **Stillness**.

Each haiku is a moment, brief yet infinite, fleeting yet timeless. Together, they weave a tapestry of reflections on life, memory, art, and the soul's restless search for meaning. Paired with whispered notes, these verses invite you to pause, breathe, and turn inward.

Haiku is the distillation of life into pure essence: the curve of a leaf, the echo of a memory, the warmth of a smile, the hush of a star-filled sky. It is as much about what is unsaid as what is written with each line carrying a breath, a silence, a small revelation.

These verses were born alongside my paintings, my long walks, my evenings of wine and music, and my mornings of mothering, loving, and remembering. Some emerged from tenderness, others from grief, and many from a quiet yearning to understand the universe within and without.

Seventy-seven haikus is a number that felt complete, like a circle that begins and ends with stillness. This book is my offering, not of answers but of mirrors. May you find yourself between the words, and in the pauses that hold them.

This is not a book to be rushed.

It is meant to be savoured like a glass of wine, slowly, gently, one sip, one page, one breath at a time.

CONTENTS

NATURE

The world begins here, in leaves, in wind, in water, in trees, in blossoms, and in seasons that remind us we belong.

This section gathers the rhythms of earth, the steady pulse beneath our feet and the quiet lessons hidden in the simplest forms of life.

These haikus remind us that we belong to something ancient, cyclical, and endlessly renewing.

I saw green barbets
Star-gazing in the daylight
A true song of hope

– On a wintry night when Ooru feels like old times

Deep woods of autumn
Either in words or colours
I long to paint you

– Celebrating the return of lost sunshine with art

Bright cherry blossoms
Hold the promises of hope
Then, now and always

– On a rather quiet Sunday

Deep winter whispers
Tall trees of misty forests
Promises of hope

– I paint and I write snubbing the chaos

Canoe by the land
Sail with the sun and the winds
Into wilderness

– Adorning the photograph with words

Short-lived butterfly
Paradoxical beauty
Teach us about life

– Awaiting sun-showers on a June day

Birch trees of autumn
Did you whisper to the winds
Of new beginnings

– On a Sunday as I painted an autumn birch forest

See a fallen star
Hiding deep in the ocean
Make thousand wishes

– A sunny February afternoon, quiet beach

Remember talking
To pretty trees in sunshine?
Feel the priceless joy

– Talk to trees

Trees in sunshine hear
The winds whispering secrets —
Guard them in their souls

– During a 'find me by the tree' time

Dainty red lilies
Bloom and wither in all its grace
Wise guests of the sun

– Obsessive lily lover

Find wild paths to tread —
Cherry blossoms & wild flowers
Make time for the woods

– On a relaxed Sunday indulged in art

Glowing rivulet
Let the cacophony flow
Leave behind stillness

– Indulging in a mid-week moment

Colours of nature
Undo the ordinary
Imposing vibrance

– Eternal flower lover

Let the heart stay warm
When leaves fall, flowers shrivel
In cold autumn winds

– Tiptoeing into the autumns,
but the rains remain

Light up the wild soul
Narrow nooks of the being
Sun-kissed sunflower

– On a Sunday of love & light

Tread the cost-free walks
Breathe, and take in the blessings
Through the wild willows

– Breathe slow

Breathe in the moment
As red & gold leaves paint the earth
Speaking autumn dreams

– On a surreal day in Kyoto
watching this autumn beauty

A golden sunshine
Hope, dreams & memories to make
Days of year anew

– First day of '24 with promises
to weave words more often

Whispers of white waves
Are you a dreamlike sunset
Or a fabled thought?

– Eye to eye with the drowning golden sun

Chasing kites & dreams
Traversing lands & seas afar
With promises to keep

– A February morning at Hanoi '24

Autumn leaf you beaut
Making a home amidst words
Memories of love

– On finding my dried leaf from Kyoto '23

Resilient beauty
With hues of charm & elegance
The sea–lavender

– On the dried sea - lavender

Is it a promise?
To paint a new dream & bring hope
Pretty spring blossoms

– Flowers bring a promise

Ocean of blossoms
Of deepest colours of life
Almost summer love

– Summer blooms

Indulge deep in life
In art, poetry & tales
Colours of your soul

– On the fifth day of 14-day water journaling

Brink of spring blossoms
Bring us hope, promise & new dreams
Stargazer lilies

– A May morning, beckoning peace

Why am I obsessed?
You're nothing more than pure joy
Little heart-stealers

– Sunshiny blooms stealing my gaze

Dhane ask'e the ir saiomtahof hanommies.
An tvomcicriso dultode smadn tore the stape,
Weinemboricnon imantinganengomas difio,
Paramo arcfiait an oluner punonbicare mude.
Uilwe ifout imont binonaustanty ofircimiter,
Cotende athor moutule hingemeneciurtioy.
Witnar omche thie mnensem bnoce Scory.
Wue lsonotip ohder airle oufitin domonenina
Luhonth tumene avme bovirey lo smanrichs.
Bevuingna and to hainive seliclaing bomierts.
Wtsaitin onove blanp mery cupe mace.
Yacnbeta thoovtuthor haiwrydileteus.

LOVE

Here, the heart softens.

Love appears in its many shades: tender, playful, aching, expansive.

These verses explore the warmth of connection, the intimacy of a glance, the comfort of presence, the wild joy of being held, and the quiet courage of holding another.

Deep beautiful eyes
Doors to her divinity
Still shines on me bright

– Amma

Sunshine at our home
Wearing a smile to light up
The littlest corners

– Ever in awe of A's smile

Drapes that emote love
Wrapped in my mother's warm hug
Long gone, yet with me

– Amma's embrace eternal

A thousand wishes
The best is being with you
Across lands and times

– Painting memories with sonny boy

Pillow of soft clouds
Carrying memories made
Lost in summer skies

– Flying back home

Bittersweet echoes
Asks for intrepidity
Love overpowers

– Listening to tales of my dad

The fondest & painful
Memories of a passed one
Wakens consciousness

– Remembering loved ones

An eternal bond
Warmth of cuddles, twinkling gazes
Whiskers of all joy

– Champagne & Merlot

Disquieted wait
Fluttering & racing of hearts
It's sunshine or rain

– A lover's face

The once little hands
Are now a boulder of strength
Anchor of my soul

– For A

Those immersive eyes
A cat's curious whisker
Measuring your soul

– Champagne & Merlot gazing at my artwork

Hold my hand for keeps
Making mistakes, evolving
Find me everyday

– For my best friend

I run out of words
To whisper of depth, truth & love
Emote in silence

– For P

SHADOWS

A journey inward always meets darkness.

This section moves through the valleys - moments of grief, doubt, longing, and the shadows that shape us just as surely as light does.

These haikus sit with the parts we often hide, offering not fear, but recognition, honesty, and depth. The shadows remind us that life is layered, fragile, and infinitely deep.

What would you do when
Grim reaper arrives home to
Your shiny plunders?

– Weigh your moves

How often are you
Touching depths of memories
Always or never

– Memories

Waltzing in my head
Are you a thought or imprint?
Make it a scarred soul

– A wretched heartache

An old wrecked building
Sealed with broken glass windows
And words on the wall

– Imperfect beauty, Malaysia

Drowning deep in dreams
Sight of grey clouds & sounds of grief
Wake me up to life

– From a sad dream

Through the racing thoughts
Pause, peek & hold on to, but one
Secret to stillness

– Let the thoughts flow

Picturesque dreams & thoughts
Painted in the mind at will
Caprice cognizance

– Caprice & desires

Gaze an old mirror
Seek verity of the now
Distorted visions

– Old mirror lies

A joyous chaos
A zillion curious eyes
Yet, you're cold & alone

– Alone in a crowd

Spewing vicious words
Spiraling hurried fury
Silence cuts deeper

– Silence after an argument

All words unspoken
A mire of shadowed longings
Alone sipping wine

– Racing thoughts in solitude

Would you help return
To the path that leads to you
Forever adrift

– The pain of losing a loved one

CREATION

From the dark comes fire. To create is to heal.

This section celebrates imagination, art, reinvention, and the brave act of becoming.

Each haiku is a spark, the beginning of a new thought, a new painting, a new self.

It is where inspiration breathes, grows, and transforms.

A sightless free fall
Into the oblivion
Yet the sacred trust

– *On trust*

A candid capture
Of balmy disposition
Mayhem in the mind

– *Mercurial thoughts*

A few or zillion
All it takes is flow of words
To waltz with the mind

– Talk to me

Open treasure troves
Drowning in the rhythms in glee
Memory ballad

– Beautiful memories for keeps

Words woven to life
Of seasons, love, joy & galaxies
Song of love letters

– Beauty of poetry

An artful vision
Spill of paint on the canvas
Born imperfect, whole

– A masterpiece in spills

Perfect morning brews
Steers the rhythm of mind & moments
Elixer of life

– On coffee

Flow of poetry
Time dissolves in ruby swirls
Aged wine in a bottle

– For Pinot Noir

Bordeaux – tinted heart
A myriad wild flowers
Standing tall with grace

– A beautiful morning blossom

UNIVERSE

Lift your gaze. The stars, the moon, the galaxies, the infinite expanse beyond thought and time. Here we are reminded of both our smallness and our vastness, a single breath in the cosmos, yet infinite within.

Craters of untruth
Verity or deception
Glow in the night sky

– Stealthy moon

A tiny being
The infinite universe
Colossal ego

– Ego

Amidst stars galore
A hunter's tale in night skies
Dreams of Orion

– On Orion

Mixed moods of the moon
Reflections of mind, heart & soul
Crescent, full & concealed

– Moon & moods

First breath of dawn breeze
Softly mending frayed hearts
Bringing back to life

– Healing dawn breeze

Gaze into vastness
Way beyond the mortal realms
One speck in the void

– Cosmic consciousness

STILLNESS

The journey ends where it began: in quiet.

This section honours the hush between breaths, the peace that comes after understanding, and the soft clarity of simply being.

It is a place of acceptance, presence, and gentle surrender - the gravity of quiet itself.

All the knocks on doors
May be curious minds or
Seeking hearts aloud

– The seek

The nightingales sing
With appearances in the dark
Midnight inspires too

– Dark could be beautiful

As cold as this night
I found myself some starlight
While clouds dance in grey

– Peace in chaos

On days of sunshine
Embrace joy & felicity
Indulge in the now

– Cognizance

Unfiltered, yet veiled —
Wonder wrapped in fine armour
Soft fire, savage heart

– Layers of a friend's heart

A thousand whispers
Fierce beats of the racing heart
Feel silence aloud

– Paradox of quiet

Million words written
Drifting through echoes, stories
Stillness on last page

– Silence is louder

Is there an end, if?
What I'm here to realise
Purpose through pain & path

– Life's quest

COFFEE

Is there an end, if?
What I'm here to realise
Purpose through pain & path

– Life's quest

COFFEE

ABOUT THE POET

Sneha is an entrepreneur whose life moves in quiet currents between creativity and contemplation. As the founder of two creative brands, Black & White Creative Studio and Kyoto, she imagines and shapes stories for brands with the same intention she brings to her poetry, with clarity, depth, and emotional resonance.

Her poetry is influenced by the meditative slowness of painting, her fascination with the unseen patterns of existence, and her instinct for surrendering to the flow of a moment. Drawn to philosophy, quantum thought, and the subtle mysteries of being, she sees poetry as a way of perceiving the world more finely, tuning into the delicate threads that bind the ordinary to the infinite.

Her haikus emerge from a place of stillness, wonder, and inner listening. They are reflections of a soul that notices the small shifts in the world, the hush of mornings, the weight of memory, the shimmer of possibility, the quiet dialogue between self and universe.

The Gravity of Quiet is her offering, a gentle constellation of being, gathered one breath, one pause, one moment at a time.